WITHDRAWN

Fungi

Elaine Pascoe

Photographs by Dwight Kuhn

The Rosen Publishing Group's
PowerKids Press ™
New York

Published in 2003 by The Rosen Publishing Group, Inc.
29 East 21st Street, New York, NY 10010

First Edition

Editor: Natashya Wilson
Book Design: Emily Muschinske
Layout Design: Eric DePalo

Photo Credits: All photographs © Dwight Kuhn, except p. 6 (inset) © Brian Kuhn/Dwight Kuhn Photography.

Pascoe, Elaine.
Fungi / Elaine Pascoe ; Photography by Dwight Kuhn.
    p. cm. — (A kid's guide to the classification of living things)
Includes bibliographical references (p.   ).
Summary: Discusses the characteristics of fungi and describes specific members of this class, including mushrooms, molds, and lichens.
  ISBN 0-8239-6313-6 (lib. bdg.)
1. Fungi—Juvenile literature. [1. Fungi.] I. Title.
  QK603.5 .P367 2003
  579.5—dc21

                                                                    2001007252

Manufactured in the United States of America

Contents

Sorting Living Things

An orange blob grows from the trunk of a dead tree. This blob is one of the thousands of types of fungi. Where does this strange growth fit in the world of living things?

Scientists use a system called classification to make sense of the great variety of life on Earth. They sort, or classify, living things into groups based on ways in which they are alike. If you collect stamps, you classify them. You put stamps from one country in one section of your album. Stamps from another country go in another section.

In the same way, most scientists sort living things into five **kingdoms**. Each kingdom is then sorted into smaller and smaller groups. This book is about one of the five kingdoms, the fungus kingdom.

The first five kingdoms into which scientists sort living things make up the top row of this diagram. The fungus kingdom is sorted into smaller groups.

**Plant
Kingdom**

**Fungus
Kingdom**

**Animal
Kingdom**

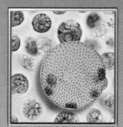

**Protist
Kingdom**

**Monera
Kingdom**

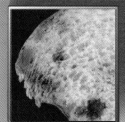

**Primitive
Fungi**

Club Fungi

Sac Fungi

Gilled Mushrooms

Puffballs

Lichens

Yeasts

Molds

**Scarlet Waxy Cap
Mushrooms**

**Lawn
Mushrooms**

The Fungus Kingdom

Mushrooms, molds, and their relatives make up the fungus kingdom. Fungi are different from other living things in many ways. Plants can make their own food, but fungi cannot. Animals move around to find food, but fungi do not. Fungi also cannot digest food inside their bodies, as animals do. Fungi feed by taking in **nutrients** from the material on which they grow. All of these traits are reasons that scientists have put fungi into a kingdom of their own.

Fungi are everywhere, but they grow best in damp places. Some fungi, such as yeasts, are so small that you need a microscope to see them. Some fungi, such as certain mushrooms, grow to be bigger than soccer balls!

Fungi come in many colors and shapes, from brown, umbrella-shaped lawn mushrooms to orange, fan-shaped shelf fungi (inset).

Many Kinds of Mushrooms

Mushrooms are fungi that grow in damp soil and in rotting wood. They may be shaped like cups, balls, umbrellas, or shelves. They may be brown, white, red, or some other color. They have so many different looks that it can be difficult to sort them based on their looks alone.

No matter what a mushroom looks like, only part of the fungus grows above ground. The rest is hidden under the soil or inside the rotting log where the mushroom grows. The hidden part is made up of tiny, white threads called **hyphae**. The hyphae give off powerful substances called **enzymes**. The enzymes break down the soil or the log so that the hyphae can soak up the nutrients.

These are the hyphae of a fungus. The hyphae can spread far and wide under the ground where the fungus grows.

How Mushrooms Grow

The mushroom is the fruit, or **fruiting body**, of the fungus. It is filled with tiny **spores** that look like specks of dust. Each spore can grow into a new fungus.

Umbrella-shaped mushrooms belong to the club fungi group. These mushrooms carry their spores in ridges called **gills** on the undersides of their caps. Round puffballs are also club fungi. They send out puffy clouds of spores from holes in their tops. Members of another fungi group, the sac fungi, carry their spores in tiny pouches. Cup-shaped mushrooms, **morels**, and **truffles** belong to the sac fungi group.

Wind, rain, and passing animals carry the spores away. If a spore lands on damp soil, it begins to grow. Threadlike hyphae grow first. Then new mushrooms push up through the soil.

 These new mushrooms have just pushed through the soil to grow above ground. Their hyphae have spread out below the soil.

These yellow fairy cup mushrooms are part of the sac fungi group.

Fungi come in many colors. These beautiful orange waxy cap mushrooms are part of the club fungi group.

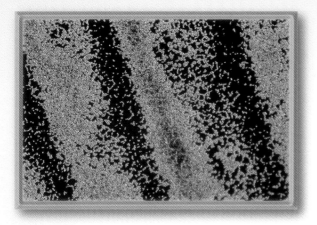

These are the tiny, black spores carried by umbrella-shaped mushrooms in their gills.

Fungi grow in many different shapes. This fungus looks a bit like sea coral.

Many club fungi carry their spores in the gills under their caps, shown here. These mushrooms are growing from a fallen log.

Yeasts: Simple Fungi

Yeasts are the simplest members of the fungus kingdom. Most fungi are made up of many **cells**. A yeast is only one cell. Yeast cells are either round or oval. Most types of yeast are sac fungi.

A yeast cell can be **dormant** for many years. In this state, the yeast cell is like a spore. The cell comes to life when it lands on a place with moisture and sugar. It grows and multiplies by **budding**. This means that part of the cell grows bigger until it breaks off. It forms another cell that is just like the first.

One kind of yeast makes bread light and fluffy. Baker's yeast is added to bread dough. As the yeast breaks down the sugar in the dough, it gives off a gas called carbon dioxide. The tiny bubbles of gas make the dough puff up, or rise.

These yeast cells are budding. On the right side of the picture, you can see a new yeast cell breaking off from its parent cell.

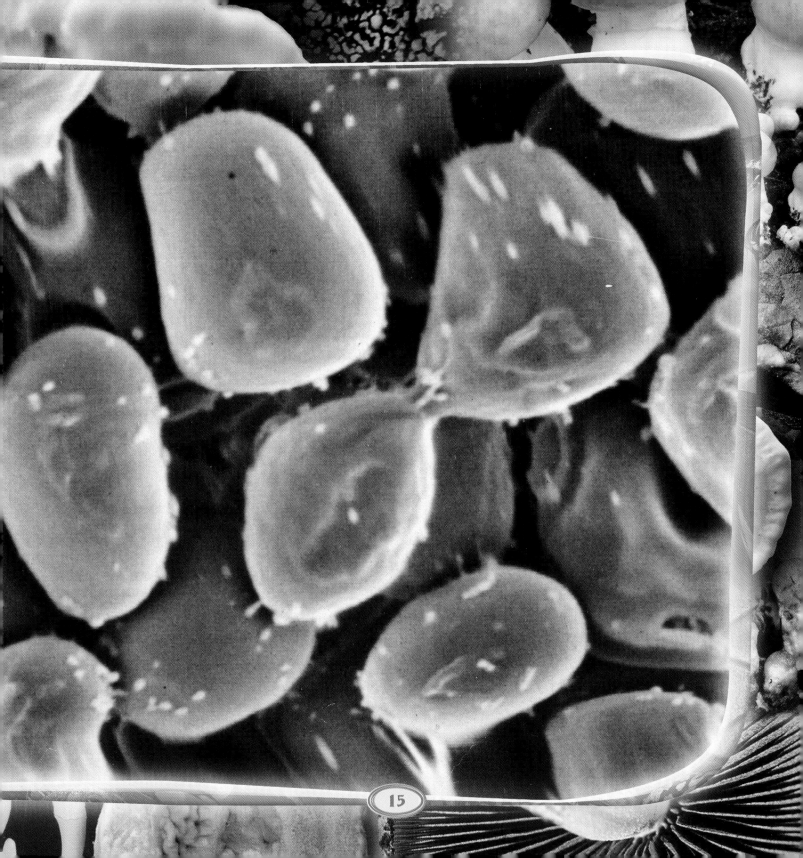

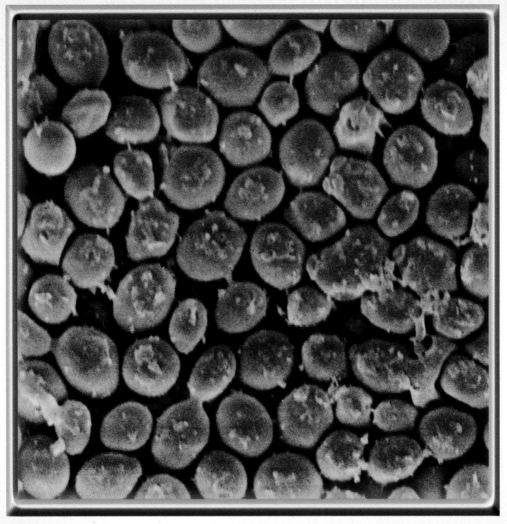

Yeasts are single-celled fungi. Some yeasts are used in making bread, cheese, and other foods. Other types can cause illnesses.

The yeast used to make bread releases gas bubbles that cause the bread to rise. The gas leaves pockets of air in the baked bread, which makes the bread light and puffy.

Molds: Spoilers

Have you ever reached for a piece of fruit and found fuzzy mold growing on it? You probably threw it away quickly! Molds are fungi that grow on bread, fruits, and other foods, as well. A mold's threadlike hyphae push into the food, break it down, and soak up nutrients. When the mold is ready to **reproduce**, it sends up thin stalks topped with tiny balls above the surface. These are the mold's fruiting bodies, and they hold its spores. The balls may be black, blue, green, or yellow. They give a mold its color and make it look fuzzy. Most molds are sac fungi, although some common bread molds belong to a separate fungi group. The fungi that people call mildew are also molds. They can grow on leather, on paper, and even on bathroom walls. Mildews grow in damp places.

You can see the round fruiting bodies in this mold, which has grown on a pumpkin.

Lichens: Partners

Lichens grow on rocks, on tree trunks, and on other bare places. Some lichens look flat and crusty. Some look leafy. Others look like feathers. Lichens are the product of one of nature's great partnerships.

Fungi team up with one-celled **organisms** called **algae** to form lichens. Algae contain materials called **pigments**. These pigments allow them to use the energy in sunlight to make food. Pigments also give algae their colors. Algae can be green, blue, orange, or many other colors.

The algae in a lichen live in the fibers of the fungus. They make enough food for the fungus and for themselves. The fungus gives the algae a sheltered place to live and helps to provide water and minerals for the algae.

 The fungus-and-algae partnership works so well that lichens can grow in harsh climates. Lichens grow in deserts and on cold mountaintops.

Bread mold is easier to see once it turns blue and black. The yellow and orange colors show where the mold has just started to grow.

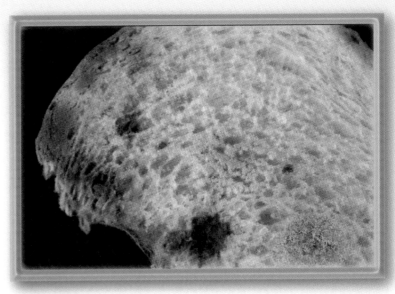

The fruiting bodies of a mold grow out of this tomato. Beneath the surface the mold's hyphae are growing through the tomato's insides.

Some lichens look like long, leafy feathers.

Other lichens look like lettuce leaves.

Fungi and Decay

All living things die at some point. After they die, they **decompose**. This means that their bodies break down into simpler parts. This process does not happen on its own. Many different organisms are decomposers. These decomposers help to break down the bodies of living things that have died.

Fungi are among the most important decomposers. They help to keep dead plants, fallen leaves, and dead animals from piling up. A fungus that grows on a dead tree breaks down the tree's wood. The fungus takes the nutrients it needs, but it leaves other nutrients. Those nutrients return to the soil as the dead tree crumbles away. In the soil, the nutrients help new plants to grow.

You can see new plants growing all around this rotting log. Fungi that live on this log are helping it to decompose.

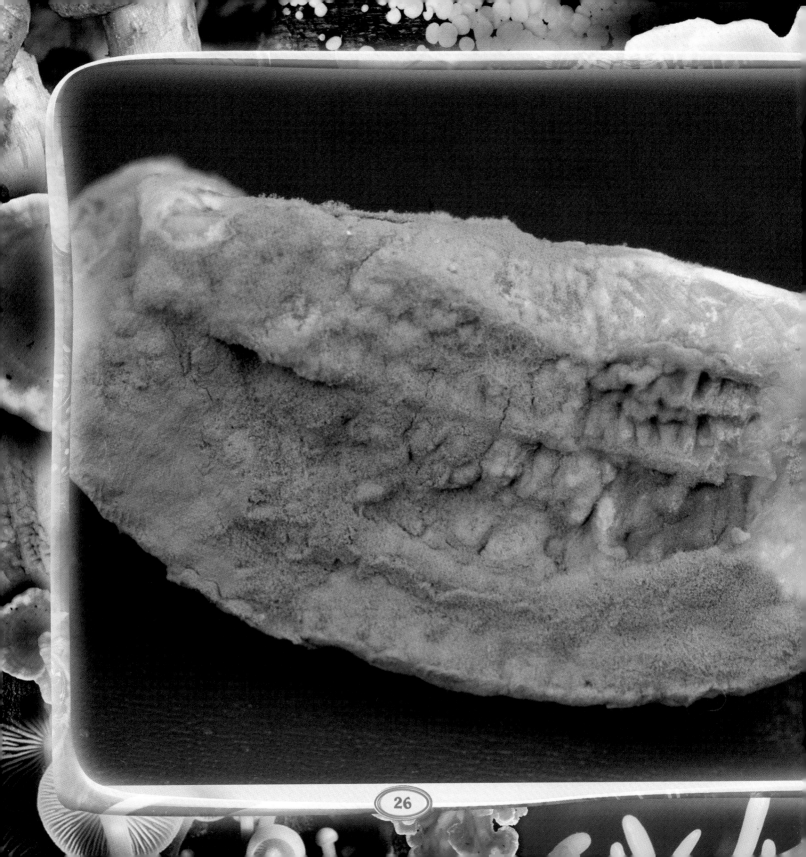

Harmful or Helpful?

Some fungi don't wait for a plant or an animal to die before they begin to grow on it. Fungi that grow in or on living things are **parasites**. They cause many diseases in plants and in animals. In people, parasitic fungi can cause annoying problems, such as athlete's foot and ringworm. They can also cause some serious diseases.

Many other fungi are helpful. Some mushrooms are poisonous, but many others are food for people and for animals. People use yeasts and other fungi to make bread, cheese, and drinks such as beer and hard cider. Some important medicines come from fungi, too. Penicillin, a drug that has saved many lives, comes from a mold.

The medicine penicillin is made from a penicillin mold, seen here growing on a lemon.

This newly fallen apple looks ripe and ready to be eaten.

Molds and other decomposers break down the apple. The remains of the apple will help new plants to grow.

These spots are a sign of early blight, a plant disease caused by a fungus.

Dutch elm disease, a disease caused by a parasitic fungus, is killing this elm tree. Since the 1930s, Dutch elm disease has killed more than half of the elm trees in North America.

Living and Nonliving

A mushroom grows beneath a tree. In the tree's branches, a bird builds a nest. The mushroom, the tree, and the bird are all different, yet they are alike in some important ways. They are living things.

Living things can reproduce, or can make more of their own kind. They grow and develop, and they use food. Plants make their own food. Other living things get their food in different ways. Living things sense the world around them and react to it. A fungus reacts to **temperature** by changing the way it grows.

This book cannot sense heat or cold. It doesn't eat, and it can't grow or make more books. These traits show us that the book is a nonliving thing.

Rocks and water do not use food or reproduce. They are nonliving things.

Glossary

algae (AL-jee) Simple living things that can make their own food.

budding (BUHD-ing) A way of reproducing in which a piece of a living thing breaks away and forms a new living thing.

cells (SELZ) Tiny units that make up all living things.

decompose (dee-kum-POHZ) To break down the cells of dead plants and animals into simpler parts.

dormant (DOR-muhnt) Resting or inactive.

enzymes (EN-zymz) Chemicals made by living things to break down food.

fruiting body (FROOT-ing BAH-dee) The part of a fungus that contains spores for making more fungi.

gills (GILZ) Soft, ridged structures on the undersides of mushroom caps.

hyphae (HY-fee) Fine threads that make up most kinds of fungi.

kingdoms (KEENG-duhmz) The first levels of groups into which scientists sort living things.

morels (muh-RELZ) Mushroomlike fungi with pitted caps.

nutrients (NOO-tree-ints) Anything that a living thing needs to live and to grow.

organisms (OR-geh-nih-zuhmz) Living things.

parasites (PAR-uh-syts) Living things that live and feed in or on other living things.

pigments (PIG-mehntz) Materials that give color and have a variety of roles inside cells.

reproduce (ree-pruh-DOOS) To have babies.

spores (SPORZ) Cells that can grow into new living things, such as fungi.

temperature (TEHM-pruh-cher) How hot or cold something is.

truffles (TRUH-fulz) Dark, mushroomlike fungi that grow underground, near the earth's surface.

Index

Web Sites

Due to the changing nature of Internet links, PowerKids Press has developed an online list of Web sites related to the subject of this book. This site is updated regularly. Please use this link to access the list:

www.powerkidslinks.com/kgclt/fungi/